The Beauty of

Nature

The Beauty of
Nature

Tanette Clendon

CONTENTS

S.No   *Pages*

Foreword   *3*

1.COCONUT MILK...*4*

   WHAT IS COCONUT MILK ? *4*
   The Benefits of Coconut Milk *4*

2.JAMAICAN CASTOR OIL *5*

   WHAT IS JAMAICAN BLACK CASTOR OIL? *5*
   THE BENEFITS OF JAMAICAN CASTOR OIL FOR HAIR GROWTH *5*
   The Benefits of Jamaican Black Castor Oil for your skin *5*
   The Benefits of Jamaican Black Castor internal

3.SAGE...*6*

   WHAT IS SAGE?...*6*
   THE BENEFITS OF SAGE FOR HAIR GROWTH *6*
   THE BENEFITS OF SAGE INTERNAL *6*

4.OLIVE OIL...*7*

   WHAT IS OLIVE OIL? *7*
   THE BENEFITS OF OLIVE OIL FOR HAIR GROWTH *7*
   THE BENEFITS OF OLIVE OIL FOR YOUR SKIN *7*

5.EUCALYPTUS OIL...*8*

   WHAT IS EUCALYPTUS OIL? *8*
   THE BENEFITS OF EUCALYPTUS OIL FOR HAIR GROWTH *8*
   THE BENEFITS OF EUCALYPTUS OIL YOUR SKIN... 8
   The Benefits of Eucalyptus oil internal...*8*

6.HEMP SEED OIL...*9*

   WHAT IS HEMP SEED OIL? *9*
   THE BENEFITS OF HEMPSEED OIL FOR HAIR GROWTH *9*

7.COCONUT OIL...*10*

   WHAT IS COCONUT OIL?..*10*
   THE BENEFITS OF COCONUT OIL FOR HAIR GROWTH..*10*
   The Benefits Of Coconut Oil for your skin *10*
   The Benefits of Coconut Oil internal..*10*

8.BLACK BERRY FRUIT EXTRACT *11*

   WHAT IS BLACK BERRY FRUIT?..*11*
   THE BENEFITS OF BLACK BERRY FRUIT FOR HAIR GROWTH *11*
   The Benefits of Black Berry Fruit internal *11*

9. GINSENG *12*

WHAT IS GINSENG? *12*
THE BENEFITS OF GINSENG FOR HAIR GROWTH *12*
The Benefits of Ginseng internal *12*

10.ALOE VERA **13**

WHAT IS ALOE VERA? *13*
THE BENEFITS OF ALOE VERA FOR HAIR GROWTH *13*
The Benefits Of Aloe Vera for your skin *13*
The Benefits of Aloe Vera internal *13*

11. ROSEMARY **14**

WHAT IS ROSEMARY OIL? 14
THE BENEFITS OF ROSEMARY OIL FOR HAIR GROWTH 14
The Benefits Of RoseMary Oil for your skin *14*

12.SHEA BUTTER **15**

WHAT IS SHEA BUTTER? *15*
THE BENEFITS OF SHEA BUTTER FOR HAIR GROWTH *15*
The Benefits Of Shea Butter for your skin *15*

13.MANGO EXTRACT **16**

WHAT IS MANGO EXTRACT? *16*
THE BENEFITS OF MANGO EXTRACT FOR HAIR GROWTH *16*
The Benefits Of Mango Extract for your skin *16*
The Benefits of Mango Extract internal *16*

14. VITAMIN B3 .... **17**

WHAT IS VITAMIN B3? 17
THE BENEFITS OF VITAMIN B3 FOR HAIR GROWTH 17
The Benefits Of Vitamin B3 for your skin 17
The Benefits of B3 internal 17

15. VITAMIN B5 .... **18**

WHAT IS VITAMIN B5? 18
THE BENEFITS OF VITAMIN B5 FOR HAIR GROWTH 18
The Benefits Of Vitamin B5 for your skin 18
The Benefits of Vitamin B5 internal 18

16.VITAMIN C **19**

WHAT IS VITAMIN C? *19*
THE BENEFITS OF VITAMIN C FOR HAIR GROWTH *19*
The Benefits Of Vitamin C for your skin *19*
The Benefits of Vitamin C internal *19*

17. VITAMIN H **20**

WHAT IS VITAMIN H? *20*
THE BENEFITS OF VITAMIN H FOR HAIR GROWTH *20*
The Benefits of Vitamin H for your skin *20*
The Benefits of Vitamin H internal *20*

18.VITAMIN E **21**

WHAT IS VITAMIN E? *21*
THE BENEFITS OF VITAMIN E FOR HAIR GROWTH *21*
The Benefits of Vitamin E for your skin *21*
The Benefits of Vitamin E internal *21*

Foreword

Tanette Clendon introduces readers to the concept of "The Beauty of Nature," a practice of doing less and allowing the elements and the life force of nature to revive the hair, body, skin, and soul so that our natural radiance can shine through. This book is a comprehensive resource for anyone who wants to simplify and educate their self-care routine, and who wants to take their health into their own hands. And also discover their own radiant beauty through the Natural sources of Nature.

Coconut milk is the liquid that comes from the grated meat of a mature coconut. The opacity and creamy taste of coconut milk is due to its high oil content, most of which is saturated fat. Coconut milk is a popular food ingredient used in Southeast Asia, South Asia, the Caribbean, and northern South America.

It's packed with vitamins C, E, B1, B3, B5, and B6 as well as iron, calcium selenium, sodium, magnesium, manganese and phosphorus. It's also a good source of proteins and natural oils. How does coconut milk help our hair? …It helps to protect our hair from the loss of protein.

Coconut milk is highly nutritious when ingested, and these nutrients may help fortify and condition the skin and hair as well. The fatty acids in coconut milk are a natural antiseptic and may help treat dandruff, skin infections, wounds, and dry itchy skin. Furthermore, the high fatty acid content in coconut milk serves as a natural moisturizer for healthy skin and may help repair wrinkles and sagging of aging skin. In addition to providing nutrients and upon its awesome taste, coconut milk contains beneficial fat called lauric acid, a medium-chain fatty acid that is quickly absorbed and used by the body for energy. Coconuts' fatty acids are primarily saturated fats but don't think these will raise your **cholesterol** levels and cause heart damage. Instead, they're known to actually do the opposite. Also, coconut milk can help you LOWER cholesterol levels, improve **blood pressure**, and prevent heart attacks or a stroke.

In addition, coconut milk is also rich in magnesium, potassium, phosphorous and iron. Magnesium is responsible for many biochemical functions in the body, including regulating the heart's rhythm and supporting the function of nerve cells. Potassium maintains the tissues of the heart, kidneys, brain and muscles. Phosphorus keeps teeth and bones strong, and also, its iron content creates a steady build-up of red blood cells and carries oxygen throughout your body. Add coconut milk to your cereal and baked goods, or drink a glass or two each day to receive these benefits.

The **Jamaican Black Castor Oil: This oil** is made from the high-quality castor beans which are gently roasted and processed to preserve its natural magnetism and balance. The **Jamaican Castor Oil** is rich in Vitamin E, Omega Fatty Acids, and Minerals.

Castor oil makes the hair fuller and shinier. It also improves the hair strength. And the Jamaican black castor oil possesses great benefits for hair growth.

The Jamaican black castor oil is rich in omega-9 fatty acid that moisturizes the hair and scalp, and it acts as best hair oil. Castor oil has more nutrients that thicken the hair. It is a fast hair growth oil. This combined with the omega-6 and 9 fatty acids, penetrates the hair shafts and roots and nourishes it, restoring its optimum health and boosting hair growth.

Castor oil is high in protein content making it very valuable to maintain hair health. Castor oil is rich in antioxidants that support the keratin in hair, making it smoother, stronger and less frizzy. This oil also can make your eyelashes and eyebrows longer and thicker.

Jamaican Castor oil is the best hair regrowth oil, and a good conditioner that treats your dull and damaged hair.

The benefit of Jamaican black castor oil on the face helps to fight signs of aging like wrinkles. The castor oil cleans your pores, thus keeping your skin healthy by preventing clogged pores. The castor oil also helps the treating of acne, the omega-9 fatty acids in Jamaican black castor oil works great for acne. The main benefit of Jamaican black castor oil is its effectiveness in treating chapped lips and healing of scars.

The Jamaican black castor oil can as well work wonders in the healing of muscle and joint pains. The castor oil pack can give a lot of relief. The castor oil also helps in the cure of insomnia. It will clean your lungs and improve your respiratory health. The oil acts also as a strong relieve from constipation.

Sage is a common spice used in kitchens all over the world. The Latin name, Salvia officinalis, means "to save," reflecting the curative properties the herb was believed to possess. Sage is a traditional topical treatment for graying hair, and the herb promotes new hair growth, according to the University of Maryland Medical Center. Sage has antibiotic, anti-allergic and antiseptic properties and is a source of magnesium, zinc, potassium, and vitamin B and C. Before using sage as a beauty treatment, consult your doctor to diagnose the cause of your thinning hair, as it could be the result of a health condition.

If you use sage tea as a hair rinse, it will add shine to your hair and fight dandruff too. To make a sage hair rinse, add boiling water to one tablespoon of dried sage in a cup and leave it to brew for a while. Strain the tea, allow it to cool and then rinse your hair with the tea; and then give it a final rinse in warm water.
Sage has a powerful anti-inflammatory effect, and it is often used to treat sore throats and other inflammations. You can use sage tea as an antiseptic mouthwash for the treatment of mouth ulcers and gum disease, or you can gargle with it to soothe sore throats.

Sage is also well known for its ability to reduce sweating. One other great health benefits of sage is that it can also be used to treat mild cases of gastrointestinal problems and dyspepsia. It has a calmative effect, which soothes indigestion and heartburn and stimulates the digestive system.

Olive oil: This oil is yet another powerhouse when it comes to hair, skin and beauty applications. Its rich, moisturizing properties make it ideal for use on your hair. While you may immediately think of olive oil for cooking, keeping a bottle of olive oil handy in your bathroom can help your hair look healthier, stronger and shinier. Whether you use it as your regular conditioner, or a hot oil treatment, and maybe as a hair finishing product, your mane is bound to reap the many benefits of olive oil. Replacing your regular conditioner with olive oil, helps bring moisture back to the hair, leaving it healthy-looking and shiny. Rich in vitamins A, E and antioxidants, olive oil helps protect the keratin in hair and seals in moisture. According to Elle, olive oil can remove the buildup of sebum that impedes the formation of new hair follicles and hinders hair growth.

If you are dealing with brittle ends or frizzy curls that feel more like steel wool than they do soft locks, olive oil can help soften your hair, making it more pliable. A natural deep conditioning treatment with olive oil each week can replace the extra silicone ingredients used in conditioners that give your hair a false feeling of softness for a few hours.

Olive oil has so many skin and health benefits. Studies have shown that the fatty acids in extra-virgin olive oil can protect your liver from oxidative stress. Research also proves that applying olive oil to the skin can prevent signs of photo-aging and sun damage. It's true—using olive oil for your skin is a sure thing. According to aesthetic plastic surgeon Paul Lorenc, MD, it's been used on skin since ancient times. "Cleopatra was a fan," says Lorenc. "Olive oil contains antioxidants that fight free-radical damage and an ingredient called squalene, which is extremely hydrating."

Olive oil contains three major antioxidants: vitamin E, polyphenols, and phytosterols. Antioxidants, when topically applied, may help protect the skin from premature skin aging. Vitamin E partly accounts for the anti-aging benefits of olive oil because it helps restore skin smoothness and protects against ultraviolet light. Hydroxytyrosol, a somewhat rare compound found in olive oil, also prevents free radical damage to the skin.

Eucalyptus Oil: Made from leaves of selected eucalyptus, also called fever tree or gum tree) are retrieved for their medicinal properties. Aside from extracting their essential oils, the bark of the eucalyptus tree is used for papermaking, and the wood in Australia is used as fuel and timber.

Eucalyptus oil has many antifungal properties that can help ward off infection, restrain residue build-up and clogging of pores on the head. Let's check out some eucalyptus oil benefits for hair;

Follicles are tiny openings from where our hairs grow. Eucalyptus oil has many chemicals that promote blood vessel constriction and cleansing. This process, in turn, promotes follicle stimulation. This stimulation promotes hair development. The basic idea circles around getting a smooth blood flow to the skin around the follicles. Eucalyptus oil improves shine, thickness, and overall health of your hair. However, too much use can actually reduce the shine and result in a greasy scalp. Most experts suggest using eucalyptus oil for the hair an hour or so before bathing, and then use a good shampoo to remove the residue, followed by a good conditioner. Eucalyptus essential oil is no doubt a proven follicle stimulant.

Eucalyptus oil is one of the best essential oils for the relieve of headaches because it may alleviate sinus pressure that can cause a lot of pain and tension. It also has invigorating properties that can boost mental clarity and promote relaxation of tense facial muscles, which is helpful when you are suffering from a headache caused by stress or exhaustion. These results seemed to be most effective and pronounced when eucalyptus oil is combined with peppermint oil and a carrier.
Eucalyptus oil has invigorating, soothing and purifying properties, which is why it can be used to boost energy and mental clarity. It may help to clear your airways, allow more oxygen into your lungs and relieve brain fog.

Hemp Seed Oil: This oil is obtained by pressing hemp seeds. Cold pressed, unrefined hemp oil is dark to clear light green in color, with a nutty flavor. The darker the color, the grassier the flavor.

There are many health benefits associated with hemp seed oil including using it to beautify the hair from inside and out. The oil is full of essential nutrients and is suitable for people of all hair and skin types, authors Lauren Cox and Janice Cox advice in their book "Ecobeauty.

Hemp oil also helps to enhance the growth of hair on the scalp in a number of ways. Among these is through the Omega-3, Omega-6 and Omega-9 fatty acids, which are necessary for stimulating growth.

Hair is made of keratin, up to 90% of which is a protein. Hemp oil can provide this protein during growth as an essential element of the hair, especially when included in a diet.

The oil also improves blood circulation on the scalp, which ensures that the hair follicles are well nourished enough to support hair growth.

It is very embarrassing to have your hair break. Fortunately, one of the hemp oil benefits for hair is strengthening.

When the hair is excessively dry, it becomes weak and breaks easily. Hemp oil can maintain hair's natural texture and makes the scalp livelier to support the hair better.

These hemp oil benefits for hair tackle the common issues experienced by many people around the world. Research published by the Journal of Agricultural and Food Chemistry validates the use of hemp oil hair products in different easy-to-use formats for improved wellness.

For healthy hair, some amount of moisture must be introduced and maintained. This is necessary especially in drier weather and climates, which tend to dry out skin and hair.

 Another significant benefit of hemp oil for hair, is its moisturizing properties. Hemp oil will prevent water loss and inject moisture into the hair and scalp.

In addition, it is quickly absorbed by the scalp and hair, so it doesn't get sticky and leave a mess.

Coconut Oil is still very popular and frequently preferred as hair oil worldwide. Before you start using this oil for its many benefits, perhaps you should find out what makes it so unique, and why millions of people choose to use it.

The use of coconut oil on your hair helps reduce protein loss in both damaged as well as undamaged hair. This oil is rich in lauric acid, has a high affinity for hair protein, and easily penetrates through the hair shaft due to its low molecular weight. It can be used for both pre-wash or post-wash hair grooming.

Coconut oil has high moisture retaining capacity as it is very stable and does not easily evaporate. It does not let moisture escape, thus keeping the hair moist and soft, which prevents hair damage.

Coconut oil is a better conditioner for hair than any synthetic one available in the market. Use of warm coconut oil helps in keeping the hair shimmering and soft. Apply some warm oil at night and wash your hair the next morning. This can be repeated every few days for healthy, strong, and conditioned hair.

The various fatty acids present in coconut oil serve as a very good anti-dandruff agents and are far better than any anti-dandruff shampoo. Regular application of coconut oil can help you get rid of dandruff forever. When mixed with lukewarm water and castor oil it can also be effective in treating dandruff. Massage the scalp and hair with this mixture for ideal results.

Coconut oil also helps in the toning of hair, especially dry hair. Apply a warm mixture of this oil and lavender essential oil on the scalp at night, then wash and rinse your hair the next morning. You may repeat this as frequently as you want until you see your desired results. If you have a lot of split ends in your hair, it is generally advised to cut them, but in case this problem appears on a small number of your hair strands, then you can use simple home remedies to solve the problem. Regularly massage of your hair with a mixture of coconut oil and almond oil for a few minutes; this will help in minimizing the split ends.

It is claimed that coconut oil is good for several skin disorders such as acne, psoriasis, and eczema. Several readers have reported this benefit. However, scientific research is ongoing in order to prove or deny these claims. Much of the research speaks of its protein content since the replacement of sick or dying cells that can occur with various skin disorders are quickly replaced by new, healthy cells. In this way, coconut oil not only treats the infection by battling the microbial bodies, they also heal the damaged or the visible marks of that skin disorder; it is a two-in-one solution.

Black Berry Fruit Extract plays a vital role in the appearance of our outer skin. Most of us fail to realize that our skin eventually reflects what we eat. A good daily supply of vital nutrients is required for a glowing and perfect skin. Blackberries are rich in Vitamin A and Vitamin C. They also offer the highest levels of some antioxidants – higher than blueberries and strawberries too. The very dark color of the fruit is proof of its high antioxidant level. As a result, it is beneficial for the skin.

Anthocyanocides and polyphenols are two antioxidants found in abundance in blackberries. These help in fighting free radicals. The collagen-forming Vitamin C and Vitamin A, make it only more appropriate for the skin. These vitamins also act as antioxidants. And the regular consumption of blackberries protects the skin against the damaging UVA and UVB rays and aids in skin cell.

Blackberries comprise more than 85% water with an abundant dose of fiber. Both of these are essential for healthy-looking skin. The consumption of blackberries detoxifies the body and maintains the elasticity of the skin.

The Vitamin C, found in blackberries, is largely responsible for collagen production and contributes to strong hair. The antioxidants help combat the harmful and damaging effects of the environment on the hair. The topical application of the fruit extract is known to add instant volume, shine and bounce to the hair.

Consuming blackberry leaves helps to get relief from excessive bleeding during menses. The fruit is also used to regulate menses and considered a uterine tonic.

Blackberries contain minerals like potassium, manganese, copper, and magnesium. Together, these help a great deal in producing white and red blood cells.

Ginseng the fleshy root has witnessed a recent rise in popularity; it has been used in traditional Chinese medicines for centuries. The English word 'ginseng' is derived from the Chinese word rénshēn, which translates to 'plant root.' The Chinese translation refers to the forked root of the ginseng plant, which resembles a person's legs. Besides being an energy stimulant and an herbal tea staple, ginseng is a powerful ingredient for hair care. Find out 3 ways in which the ingredient can boost your hair care routine.

Ginseng is believed to increase the dermal cells on the scalp which, in turn, strengthens the follicles and roots of the hair. This not only encourages the new growth of strands but also prevents hair thinning and breakage.
If it is those unsightly white flakes that are getting you down, ginseng might be your answer. The root is high in Saponin, an anti-bacterial compound, which will sweep away dandruff from the scalp and prevent it from reoccurring. This ensures that your follicles stay clean and flake-free.

Ginseng is a herbal plant that helps both, the roots and lengths of the hair. The simplest way to make the best of this coveted ingredient is by getting your hands on the Detox & Restore Shampoo and Conditioner. This range combines the magic of ginseng with neem to create a botanical blend like none other. It cleanses the scalp of build-up and restores cuticles from the brink of damage to get manageable, nourished tresses.

The benefit of ginseng for a healthy hair, Ginseng contains volatile oil and fitoserol, with both of these substances being very useful in the prevention of awkward hair color, or early graying of the hair. The content serves as an antidote to free radicals (one of the causes of gray hair) other factors than age. As we know, free radicals are the consequences that we have to face in this modern life, especially for urban communities. With the help of ginseng, gray hair can be prevented as early as possible.

The **Aloe Vera Plant** is about one or two feet tall with prickly and bitter leaves, which act as a defense to keep animals and insects from feeding on the plant. The leaves hold a gooey translucent gel, also extremely bitter, and known all over the world for its unbelievable healing properties. This translucent gel is made up of around 96% water, some organic and inorganic compounds, a type of protein which contains 18 of the 20 amino acids found in the body and lastly, Vitamin A, B, C and E. Another part of the Aloe Vera plant which is used is the 'sap', a yellow-colored liquid stuck to the skin of the plant from the inside. When dried and purified, the powdered aloe is often used as a laxative, though it is effectiveness is questionable. Aloe Vera is extensively used in beauty products and for a good reason. It's got antiviral and antibacterial properties, and the ability to help treat everything from constipation to diabetes. The green-cactus looking plant that sits out in your garden isn't just a plant with its roots in folklore; it's the crux of a million dollar industry that extends from beauty creams to healthy juices and diet supplements. Over time, Aloe Vera has seamlessly integrated itself into everything we use. But what makes this miracle plant so distinguishable.

Aloe Vera contains something called proteolytic enzymes which repairs dead skin cells on the scalp. It also acts as a great conditioner and leaves your hair all smooth and shiny. It promotes hair growth, prevents itching on the scalp, reduces dandruff and conditions your <u>hair</u>. Diane Gage, author of Aloe Vera: Nature's Soothing Healer says, "Keratin, the primary protein of hair, consists of amino acids, oxygen, carbon, and small amounts of hydrogen, nitrogen, and Sulphur. Aloe Vera has a chemical makeup similar to that of keratin, and it rejuvenates the hair with its own nutrients, giving it more elasticity and preventing breakage."

Bill C. Coats writes, "Since the skin needs nutrition of its own, Aloe Vera, when formulated into a properly designed personal care regimen, can treat, exfoliate, restore, reveal and provide constant, impressive nutrition to the human skin." And we're about to show just how you can do that. Once you move past the slimy texture of natural Aloe Vera gel and apply it to your skin, you'll notice how soothing and cooling it is. And it's for these exact reasons that Ayurveda refers to Aloe Vera as the miracle herb that can be used to treat wounds, minor cuts, dry skin and severe burns.

Rosemary, also known as *Rosmarinus officinalis*, is very popular in the Mediterranean region as a culinary herb. Many dishes are cooked with rosemary oil and its freshly plucked leaves. Rosemary essential oil is extracted from the leaves. The rosemary bush belongs to the mint family which includes basil, lavender, myrtle, and sage.

Did you know, though, that rose essential oil, which is distilled from fresh Damascus roses has some fantastic health benefits too? Rose essential oil is an antiseptic, an antispasmodic, an aphrodisiac and an antidepressant too, so read on, and find out more about the incredible benefits of rose essential oil.

You probably won't find a sweeter smelling antiseptic than rose essential oil. Applying rose oil to minor wounds will stop infections and help them to heal quicker and, it won't have the nasty smell that some do. One other wonderful thing about rose essential oil benefits is that it can help relieve anxiety and stress. Like all essential oils, rose oil is very strong and it should be mixed with a carrier oil, and it is not usually taken internally without being well diluted. However, when it is applied to the skin, it is quickly absorbed by the body. Research has shown that people who apply rose oil to their skin felt more relaxed and calm and it can be used to treat the symptoms of anxiety and stress.

Rosemary oil and rosemary tea are widely used for hair care products like shampoos and lotions. Regular use of rosemary oil helps stimulate follicles, making the hair grow longer and stronger. It is also believed that rosemary oil slows down premature hair loss and graying of the hair. Therefore, it is an excellent tonic for bald people or for those who are beginning to show signs of male pattern baldness. Rosemary essential oil is also beneficial for dry and flaky scalps. Regular massaging of the scalp with rosemary oil nourishes the scalp and removes dandruff. Furthermore, it is often mixed with tea tree oil and basil oil to alternately treat scalp problems. For many years, Rosemary has been combined with olive oil as a way to darken and strengthen hair by using hot oil treatments. Rosemary has a mesmerizing aroma, which makes rosemary essential oil an excellent inhalant. The oil is used in room fresheners, cosmetics, beauty aids, foods, bath oils, candles, and perfumes because of its unique and intoxicating aroma. When the oil is inhaled, it can boost mental energy and is also known to clear the respiratory tract.

Shea Butter is an oil rich in fats, which is derived from the karite tree (also known as the shea tree). This oil is your solution for many skin, health, and hair health issues. Fairly recently, this butter has gained huge popularity in the western world due to its widespread use in several beauty products, such as lotions, cosmetics, shampoos, and conditioners. Let's learn more about shea butter benefits, nutritional facts and much more.

The Karite tree bears the fruits, and the nuts inside the fruits are of prime importance. These nuts are crushed, boiled, and manipulated to extract a light-colored fat, which is commonly referred to as shea butter.

The main components of shea butter include oleic acid, stearic acid, linoleic acid, etc. It gets absorbed quickly into the skin as it melts at body temperature. Its moisturizing and healing properties prove beneficial for many skin issues. It also has anti-inflammatory and antimicrobial properties (to a certain extent) that can be utilized to treat many ailments. Its similarity too many vegetable oils makes it suitable for ingestion.

A number of chemical treatments like straighteners, perms, and curlers are responsible for stripping off the natural moisture from the hair. Shea butter can help restore this lost moisture. It also protects the hair from harsh weather conditions and the harmful free radicals in the air and water. Moreover, shea butter has a low SPF that is sufficient to protect the hair from sun damage caused due to exposure to ultraviolet radiation. It repairs the damage that has already been caused by the harsh weather and the sun. This is mainly as a result of when absorbed, shea butter coats the hair shaft so that it is protected from a heat tool or any other damaging material being passed along the hair. This is particularly beneficial for processed or colored hair. It also protects the hair against salt and chlorine when applied before swimming

Shea butter is an excellent moisturizer for the face and the body. Its fat content is responsible for its emollient and humectant properties. It locks in the moisture in the skin and keeps it hydrated for long. Dehydrated and dry skin becomes rough and scaly, and certain areas of the body can even develop skin cracks due to dryness. Shea butter can nourish the skin with its fat content. It can also help to soften the skin on your hands and feet, making them supple. It penetrates the skin easily, without clogging the pores, and is effective for dry skin.

Mango Extract is one of the powerhouses of the fruit world, and they are packed full of vitamins and antioxidants that bring many, many health benefits too. Here are just twenty of those health benefits that you get from eating mango fruit.
Mangos are very rich in fiber, which improves the digestion and increases the metabolic rate; this makes mango a great fruit to eat when you are trying to lose weight.

Mangoes are also a rich source of folic acid, which is the form of Vitamin B that doctors recommend that women take when pregnant, to help keep the unborn baby healthy and happy.
People with diabetes can gain some benefit from eating mangoes too because the fruit is known to control the blood sugar levels and normalize insulin levels in the blood.

You can use a mango scrub to exfoliate your skin and remove blackheads. Mix some mango pulp with half a teaspoon of yogurt and some honey and rub it over the affected area, in a circular motion, and the mixture will exfoliate, cleanse and nourish your skin.

Mango is often used as an ingredient in commercial hair conditioners, but here's a way to make your own homemade mango hair mask. Pulp the flesh of one mango and mix it with one egg yolk, a teaspoon of honey and a spoonful of natural yogurt. Apply to your hair and leave it in for about thirty minutes before washing out.
Eating mangos can help keep your eyes healthy and fight off the onset of macular degeneration. The fruit is also a good source of Vitamin A, which is needed by the body to maintain good vision. The tartaric acid and malic acid, found in mangos, help to maintain a healthy alkaline level in the body, which helps to prevent chronic illnesses, such as kidney disease and weakening of the bones. Maintaining healthy alkaline levels also helps with the transfer of oxygen throughout the body, so it can also provide you with extra energy. Mangoes are good for your love life too. They contain a high content of Vitamin E, which can boost stamina. They also contain potassium and magnesium, which are essential ingredients in the production of the 'love' hormones.

Vitamin B3- Niacin amide, Vitamin B3 is a fantastic multi-tasker and has a lot of benefits for your skin. It helps reduce wrinkles, reduce uneven skin tone, help heal acne and reduce hyperpigmentation. A lot of research has been done on this powerful little vitamin which proves this ingredient should be part of your skincare arsenal.

Also called vitamin B3, this nutrient is water-soluble and found in several common foods like meat, tuna fish, seeds, mushrooms, etc. It is a part of the B-complex vitamins, which also include thiamine (vitamin B1), riboflavin (vitamin B2), and others.

Niacin is the medical name of vitamin B3 and comes in 3 forms – nicotinic acid, niacin amide (also called nicotinamide), and inositol hexaniacinate. It is an important vitamin and benefits one in several ways – right from protecting the heart and improving metabolism to enhancing brain function and aiding diabetes treatment.

Nicotinic acid works as a supplement and is used to treat high blood cholesterol and heart disease. Niacin amide can help treat type 1 diabetes, certain skin conditions, and schizophrenia (it doesn't lower cholesterol, though). Hence, certain forms of niacin offer you certain benefits.

Niacin is known to boost the water content in the skin, and this can be achieved by topically applying nicotinamide cream. The cream was also found to help treat acne.

Niacin also has beneficial effects for rosacea, which is a skin condition that causes red facial skin, flushing, pustules, and red bumps.

Niacin is also known to have a beneficial effect on skin cancer. Studies have shown that it can prevent premalignant cells from becoming malignant. And talking about anti-aging, niacin does play its part too. One study showed that topical niacin amide helped reduce fine lines and wrinkles and other issues with skin elasticity concerned with aging.

Vitamin B5: This keeps skin healthy and supplement, and provides key nourishment to hair follicles to promote growth. Raising "good" HDL cholesterol levels while significantly lowering "bad" LDL cholesterol levels, B5 acts as a synthesizer of lipids, proteins, carbohydrates, and amino acids essential for cell growth. Studies have also shown that Vitamin B5 plays an important role in the pigmentation of hair and prevents it from losing its color until you are well into your older years. Known as the "anti-stress" vitamin, B5 supports adrenal gland health and helps to keep stress levels in balance.

Vitamin B5 is a stimulator and balances hormones in the whole body. This function helps protect the pigmentation of hair follicles and also keeps the skin looking tighter and healthy looking for longer. A healthy intake of vitamin B 5 has shown properties of reducing the appearance of wrinkles and age spots on the face.

Vitamin B5 is also water soluble like all other vitamin B derivatives. All vitamins help the human body in converting carbohydrates into energy and even breaking down fats. Vitamin B5 is essential for a healthy functioning nervous system throughout the whole body and the brain as well.

The human body requires vitamin B5 every step of the way, in order to synthesize cholesterol and keep up the metabolic process. Vitamin B5 can be found in multivitamins and also B complex supplements; you can easily find it over the counter. The medications come under the name under calcium pantothenate and pantothenic acid.

The body needs a robust immune system to keep diseases at bay; vitamin B5 is a facilitator in almost all the important mechanisms that the body carries out to ensure a healthy functioning mind and body. Further research is being carried out to understand the impact of vitamin B5 on the increase of white blood cells.

Vitamin B5 has stimulating properties that help regulate the release of hormones from different glands in the body and ensures they are balanced and performing their necessary tasks. Vitamin B5 is a synthesizer of multiple enzymatic processes in the body including the stimulation of hormones.

Vitamin C -Our hair follicles often get clogged due to dandruff, dry, and flaky skin. This can damage the hair follicles and also inhibit hair growth. Vitamin C helps fight the bacteria on the scalp. It wards off dandruff, and helps in getting rid of the follicles' debris and encourages the growth of new hair. It also helps with dry and itchy scalps because of its antiviral properties.

Low intake of Vitamin C may be the cause of a number of hair-related problems that affect our hair growth. Vitamin C deficiency may result in dry hair and split ends. These conditions are unfavorable for the regular growth of hair and eventually lead to hair loss.

When our body turns food that we consume into glucose for energy production, free radicals are naturally formed. These free radicals damage our hair by making it weak, brittle, and thin, which interrupts hair growth. Vitamin C's antioxidant properties reduce the formation of free radicals and minimize their effect on our body. Having an adequate supply of Vitamin C in our diet is essential for antioxidant protection against free radicals.

People who take tremendous amount of vitamin C have healthy, strong, and thick hair.

Fruits and vegetables are the best sources of Vitamin C. You won't really require Vitamin C supplements as Vitamin C is already available in ample amounts in food sources and you can get the recommended amount of Vitamin C by incorporating those foods in your diet.

Citrus fruits like oranges, grapefruit, and their juices, as well as red and green pepper and kiwi fruit, contain a large content of Vitamin C. Other fruits and vegetables which include Vitamin C are broccoli, strawberries, cantaloupes, baked potatoes and tomatoes.

Vitamin H – This Vitamins (Biotin) health benefits include supporting proper metabolic function, lowering blood sugar level, supporting skin health, promoting stronger nails, treating multiple sclerosis, supporting a healthy pregnancy, promoting healthy hair, managing diabetes, relieving muscle cramps, and balancing cholesterol levels.

Vitamin H is known as Biotin, which belongs to the family of B-vitamins. It is also known as vitamin B7, or co-enzyme R. Biotin is a water-soluble vitamin, so it dissolves in your body rapidly. Although its deficiency is rare, but it should be present in your diet as it helps in various bodily functions. It is also known to promote the production of fatty acids and glucose. You can obtain it from natural sources that are super safe and easy to get. It does not contain harmful effects, however; it is suggested to consume vitamin H supplements after consulting with your physician.

Getting thick and long locks isn't a dream anymore as you can change the condition of your hair by consuming biotin. It is one of those vitamins that are recommended by beauticians to treat severe hair loss. Due to its rejuvenating qualities, high-end brands add it to their hair products. Moreover, biotin deficiency could be a reason behind chronic hair loss and supplements made with biotin can fix this condition within few weeks. Not only does vitamin H make your hair strands thick and strong, but it also helps promote rapid hair growth as well.

It is an essential vitamin to enhance the condition of your skin. Biotin is a safe source to treat some skin problems including premature wrinkles. Moreover, vitamin H does not only help in fighting the symptoms of acne, but it also prevents acne reoccurrence. It has a capability to keep your skin young regardless of your age. It has anti-aging properties that are essential to eliminate wrinkles. This is why it has been a part of well-known beauty products for years. Since it contains a healing and moisturizing component, it has become an essential part of many massage oils. If you want flawless skin, biotin is undoubtedly a health-friendly way.

 Several studies have concluded that biotin strengthens nails if 2.5 mg of the vitamins is regularly taken for 7-14 days. Hence, maintaining strong and beautiful nails is another reason to consume biotin enriched diet. Incorporating a diet rich in vitamin H is essential for your metabolic function. It is responsible for processing nutrients such as carbohydrates and protein.

Vitamin E: This class of Vitamin is best known for its <u>antioxidant properties</u> that help reduce free radical damage and protect the body's cells. Although you can find it in the supplement aisle, many companies add vitamin E to their beauty products. Vitamin E is a fat-soluble and anti-inflammatory vitamin which is chemically known as Alpha-Tocopherol. This special vitamin offers a variety of beauty and health benefits. Vitamin E is an exceptional antioxidant that helps to rebuild and repair aged tissues. When this vitamin is applied on the scalp, it helps repair damaged follicles and reduces inflammation, so that later healthy follicles can freely promote hair growth. Vitamin E is available both in the form of pills, shampoo and dietary supplements in all the leading drugstores around the world. This vitamin has gone popular with time as one of the best hair care vitamins, so let's see how well it can work for your hair.

With multiple benefits, vitamin E can be one good solution to all your hair problems. As we all know that a healthy scalp is the main foundation of a better health hair and beauty, this health benefit will promote hair growth and will also stop hair loss. There are a number of things that determine the health of a scalp such as oil production, pH levels, follicle health and circulation of blood towards the scalp. Using vitamin E can help you balance these different variables, ensuring that your hair grows strong and healthy along with offering many other following benefits:

Not to ignore, the main reason behind hair fall is imbalanced pH levels or excessive production of oil on the scalp. Such scalp issues can cause excess hair loss that may result into thinning hair, baldness or alopecia. With a lot of dryness on the scalp, the sebaceous glands go into overdrive and start producing excess oil than usual. This excess oil starts to block the hair follicles, resulting in dandruff and itching, and at the end hair fall. Vitamin E oil is a hair care product that can provide necessary moisture to the scalp and will also calm the over-excited sebaceous glands while beautifully balancing the pH levels.

Vitamin E has one strong emollient property of conditioning the hair, and it is extremely good at locking moisture in the shaft of the hair, and providing maximum conditioning. Using vitamin E regularly can eliminate dryness, resulting in strong and smooth hair. Nowadays, vitamin E can be found in many known shampoos, conditions and other hair care products. Vitamin E is known as one of the finest and rich antioxidants that can help neutralize free radicals that mainly cause damage to hair and scalp. Such use of this vitamin will keep your hair follicles free from any damage, while fighting breakage and split-ends. Vitamin E capsules can be used to take benefit from this antioxidant activity.

Using vitamin E can broaden the blood vessels that will make the circulation of blood smooth and will also prevent it from clotting. A soft vitamin E massage on the scalp can ensure improved blood circulation along with better optical nourishment towards the hair follicles. This therapy will help the follicles to work more efficiently while promoting better hair growth. Taking vitamin E pills or tablets can also help you regulate blood circulation in your body.

Back Cover wording

Nature is defined as the natural Earth and the things on it, or the essence of a person or thing. The trees, forests, birds and animals are all an example of nature. Beauty is the quality or aggregate of qualities in a person or thing that gives pleasure to the senses or pleasurably exalts the mind ,Body or spirit : loveliness.